OUR DESERT HOME

by Judy Nayer

illustrated by Tiphanie Beeke

McGraw-Hill School Division

New York   Farmington

prickly pear
cactus

joshua tree

The desert is a home.

century plant

saguaro
cactus

claret cup
cactus

beaver-tailed
cactus

barrel
cactus

The desert is home to plants.

wasp

cactus fly

butterfly

honey bee

beetle

ants

The desert is home to insects.

bull snake

gila monster

rattlesnake

gecko

lizard

tortoise

The desert is home to reptiles.

The desert is home to birds.

The desert is home to mammals.

The desert is home to me!